OneNote® for Windows® 10 Introduction

TEACHUCOMP, INC.®

Quick Reference Guide

Comprehensive video training & instruction manuals available at www.teachucomp.com

The OneNote Environment

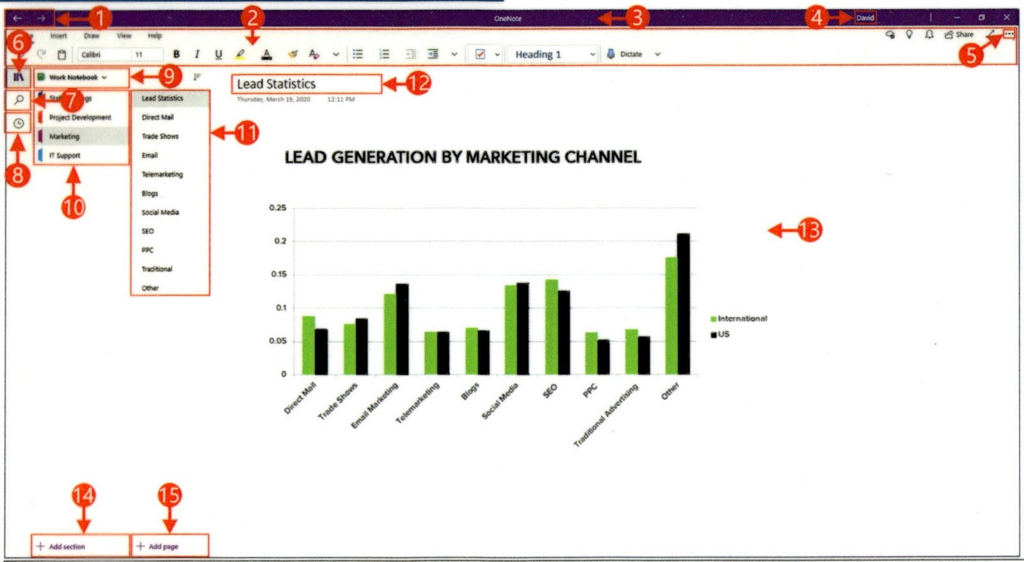

1. Backward/Forward
2. The Ribbon
3. Title Bar
4. Microsoft Account Information
5. Settings and More
6. Notebook Navigation
7. Search
8. Recent Notes
9. Notebooks List
10. Sections
11. Pages
12. Page Title Box
13. Content Pane
14. Add Section
15. Add Page

Interface Basics

About OneNote

OneNote is a digital note taking app that allows users to record, gather, organize, and store information in different formats including text notes, drawings, screen clippings, and audiovisual recordings. OneNote also offers collaborative features to share notes with other OneNote users over the internet or a network. OneNote stores information in notebooks, which are divided into sections, and sections into pages. Notebooks are easily navigated and searched to quickly locate information. Microsoft publishes OneNote as a free, stand-alone app for macOS, Windows 10, iOS, and Android, as well as a web-based version as part of Office for the web. This guide covers OneNote for Windows 10.

Using the Ribbon

1. **To hide and show the contents in the Ribbon**, click the active tab in the Ribbon.
2. **To change button groups shown in the Ribbon**, click the tabs at the top of the Ribbon.
3. **To show or hide "Contextual" tabs (hidden tabs that contain item-specific options when certain objects such as images and tables are selected)**, click to select or click away to de-select the object.
4. **To access commands**, click a Ribbon tab and use the buttons, boxes and menus within the command groups of the active tab.

Using Full Screen Mode

Full Screen mode maximizes the OneNote workspace by hiding most of the content of the Ribbon, notebook navigation commands, and Windows taskbar. **To enter Full Screen mode**, click the "Enter Full Screen Mode" button at the right end of the Ribbon. **To exit Full Screen mode**, click the "Exit Full Screen Drawing" button that appears at the right end of the modified Ribbon.

Changing OneNote Options

1. Click the "Settings and More" button at the right end of the Ribbon.
2. Select "Settings" from the menu that appears.
3. Select the "Options" category in the "Settings" pane.
4. Make changes, which are saved automatically.
5. **To close the Settings pane**, click outside of it.

Notebook Management Basics

About Notebook Navigation

Notebook management and navigation are performed in the navigation panes at the left of the application. The navigation panes can be temporarily hidden to increase workspace. Click the "Navigation" button **to toggle the panes on** or **off.** The Notebooks List displays the current active notebook and any other open notebooks.

Creating New Notebooks

1. Click the Notebooks List drop-down button.
2. Click the "Add Notebook" button at the bottom of the pane.
3. Enter a name in the "Notebook name" field.
4. Click the "Create Notebook" button.

Saving Notebooks

OneNote is different from other Microsoft applications such as Word and Excel in that OneNote automatically saves changes as you make them and syncs your notebooks to the cloud. *There is no need to save manually.* **To change sync settings:**

1. Click the "Settings and More" button.
2. Select "Settings" from the menu that appears.
3. Select the "Options" category in the "Settings" pane.
4. Make desired changes.

Closing Notebooks

1. **To close a notebook**, click the Notebooks List drop-down button.
2. Right-click on the desired notebook and select the "Close This Notebook" command.

Opening

By default, ... ere working on ...

1. **To naviga...** Notebooks List drop-down button and select the desired notebook from the list.
2. **To open a notebook**, click the Notebooks List drop-down button and select the "More Notebooks" command at the bottom.
3. Select the notebook(s) to open in the "Notebooks to open" window and click the "Open" button.

Navigating Sections and Pages

Notebooks contain sections, which are like dividers in a binder. Sections are comprised of pages (and sub-pages), which contain the notebook content.

1. **To navigate to a section**, click the section's tab under the Notebooks List drop-down.
2. **To navigate to a page**, click the page's tab that appears to the right of the selected section.
3. **To go back to the previous section, page or notebook**, click the "Back" button above the Ribbon. **To go forward *after* going back**, click the "Forward" button.

Renaming Sections and Pages

1. **To rename a section**, right click on the section tab and choose "Rename Section" from the menu. Type a name, and press the "Enter" key.
2. **To rename a page**, select the text in the "Page Title" box ***or*** right-click on the page tab and choose "Rename Page," then type a new name.

Adding a New Section or Page

1. Click the "Add section" or "Add page" button at the bottom of the Notebooks List. ***Or*** for a new page, right-click an existing page tab and select "New Page Below" from the menu.
2. Type a name, and press "Enter."

Deleting a Section or Page

1. Right-click on the section or page tab and select "Delete Section" or "Delete Page" from the menu.
2. **To confirm the deletion of a section**, select "Yes."

To restore a deleted section or page:

1. Click the "Deleted Notes" button on the "View" tab.
2. Right-click the section or page, select "Restore To," then a location, and click "Restore."

Moving or Copying a Section or Page

Moving Within the Same Notebook:

1. **To move a section**, click, drag and release the section's tab in the sections list.
2. **To move a page**, click, drag and release the page's tab in the page list to its new location. **To select multiple pages**, hold down the "Control" key while clicking to select the page tabs.
3. **To move a page to a different section**, click and drag the page's tab and *hover* over the new section's tab in the sections list until it opens. Continue dragging into the pages list and release the mouse when the page is in the desired location.

Moving or Copying to a Different Notebook:

1. Right-click on the section or page tab and choose the "Move/Copy" command from the menu.
2. **To select a different notebook**, click the arrow and make a selection.
3. Select the section and click either "Move" or "Copy."

TeachUcomp, Inc.

www.teachucomp.com

info@teachucomp.com

877.925.8080

Note Creation & Manipulation

Understanding Notes

Each piece of content added to a OneNote page is referred to as a "note." Each note (text, image, photo, drawing, screen clipping, etc.) is placed in its own separate note container, which can be moved and resized. Note containers appear when you hover over them with the mouse pointer or when you click on a page and begin typing a note.

Creating Text Notes

1. Click anywhere on an open page and type.

Copying and Pasting Note Content

1. Select the content to copy.
2. Hold down the "Control" key and then press the "C" key (to copy) or "X" key (to cut). ***Or***, click the "Cut" or "Copy" button in the "Clipboard" group or drop-down on the "Home" tab in the Ribbon of a Microsoft application (OneNote, Word, Excel, etc.).
3. In OneNote, click in the page where the content is to be placed.
4. Hold down the "Control" key and then press the "V" key. ***Or***, click the "Paste" button in the "Clipboard" drop-down on the "Home" tab in the Ribbon.
5. For paste options, select a choice from the "Paste Options" toolbar that appears at the bottom of the pasted content.

Moving Notes on a Page

1. Hover over the dark gray top edge of the note container until a four-sided arrow appears.
2. Click, drag and release the note in the new location.

Deleting Notes

1. Hover over the dark gray top edge of the note container until a four-sided arrow appears.
2. Right-click on the top edge and choose "Delete" from the menu. ***Or***, click the *top edge* of the note container to select it and press the "Delete" key.

Resizing Notes

1. **To adjust the size of a text note vertically**, press the "Enter" key at the end of a line of text.
2. **To adjust the size of a text note horizontally**, hover the mouse over the right edge of the note container until a double-sided arrow appears. Click, drag and release.
3. **To adjust the size of an image**, click the image to select it. Then, click and drag one of the corner resizing handles.

Merging Notes

The contents of two or more notes can be merged together.

1. Hover over the dark gray top edge of the note container until a four-sided arrow appears.
2. Press and hold the "Shift" key.
3. Click, drag and release the note over another note.

Selecting Multiple Objects

Select multiple objects or note containers to apply formatting as a bulk edit or to copy or move content together.

To select multiple objects on the same page:

1. Click and drag with the default type tool to fully encompass the desired objects.
2. Release the mouse when done.

To select multiple objects with greater precision:

1. Click the "Draw with Mouse or Touch" button on the "Draw" tab in the Ribbon, if necessary.
2. Click the "Lasso Select" button in the Ribbon.
3. Click and drag to fully encompass the objects to select them.
4. Release the mouse when done.

To select all objects on a page:

1. Hold down the "Control" key and then press the "A" key.

Formatting Text & Paragraphs

Using the Contextual Menus

Contextual menus contain item-specific options. **To access a contextual menu:**

1. Right-click an item (text, picture, shape, etc.). ***Or***, for touch interface, touch and hold until a box appears.
2. Click or tap to select the option from the menu.

Formatting Text

1. Select the text to change.
2. Select the "Home" tab in the Ribbon.
3. **To change the font**, click the arrow to the right of the "Font" drop-down and select a font. Calibri
4. **To change the font size**, click the arrow to the right of the "Font Size" drop-down and select a size, ***or*** type a value in the box and then press the "Enter" key. 11
5. **To apply a font color**, click the arrow to the right of the "Font Color" button and select a color.
6. **To apply bold, italics, and underline,** click the desired buttons. Click again to un-apply. B I U
7. **To apply subscript, superscript, or strikethrough,** click the "Font Formatting" drop-down and make a selection. x_2 x^2 ~~ab~~
8. **To apply a highlight**, click the arrow to the right of the "Highlight" button and select a color (or select "No Color" to un-apply).

Formatting with the Mini Toolbar

The Mini Toolbar provides quick access to many common formatting options. When the Mini Toolbar appears, click any of the available formatting options.

To access the Mini Toolbar:

1. Select text with a mouse. ***Or,***
2. Right-click text, cells or shapes. ***Or,***
3. Tap already-selected items.

To view or hide additional options, click the "Show More/Show Less" button at the right end.

Using the Format Painter

Use the Format Painter to copy and paste formatting from one selection to other selections.

1. Select the text that has the formatting to copy. **To copy paragraph formatting such as alignment**, select the entire paragraph.
2. **To apply formatting to a selection**, click the "Format Painter" button on the "Home" tab in the Ribbon.
3. Click, drag and release over the text area to which to apply the formatting.

To apply formatting to *multiple* selections using the functionality of the Format Painter:

1. Select the text that has the formatting to copy.
2. Press the "Ctrl"+"Shift"+"C" keys.
3. Select the text area to which to apply the formating.
4. Press the "Ctrl"+"Shift"+"V" keys. Repeat on other text areas, as desired.

Using Undo and Redo

1. **To undo your last action**, click the "Undo" button at the left end of the Ribbon.
2. **To redo the last action you have undone**, click the "Redo" button at the left end of the Ribbon.

Applying Styles to Text

1. Select the text.
2. Click the arrow to the right of the "Styles" drop-down on the "Home" tab of the Ribbon and make a selection. Heading 1
3. **To remove a style and apply the default font**, select "Normal" from the drop-down.

Clearing All Text Formatting

To remove text formatting and apply the default font:

1. Select the text with formatting applied.
2. Click the "Clear All Formatting" button on the "Home" tab in the Ribbon.

Changing the Default Font

1. Click the "Settings and More" button at the right end of the Ribbon. ···
2. Select "Settings" from the menu that appears.
3. Select "Options" and scroll down to "Default Font."
4. Make changes, which are saved automatically.
5. **To close the Settings pane**, click outside of it.

Changing Paragraph Alignment

1. Select the paragraph text to align.
2. Click the "Paragraph Formatting" drop-down on the "Home" tab in the Ribbon.
3. Select an alignment choice.

Changing Paragraph Indentation

1. Select the paragraph text.
2. Click the "Decrease Indent" or the "Increase Indent" button on the "Home" tab in the Ribbon.

Creating Bulleted or Numbered Lists

To create a bulleted or numbered list:

1. Select the paragraph(s).
2. Click the drop-down arrow to the right of either the "Bullets" or "Numbering" button on the "Home" tab in the Ribbon.
3. Click to select a bullet or numbering format. **To remove bullets already applied to text**, choose "None."

To create a bulleted list before typing:

1. Click the drop-down arrow to the right of the "Bullets" button on the "Home" tab in the Ribbon, select a bullet style, and begin typing. ***Or***, begin the paragraph by typing an "AutoFormat as You Type" symbol, then the spacebar.
2. Press the "Enter" key twice to complete the list.

Symbol	***Creates This Bullet***
*	●
-	-

To create a numbered list before typing:

1. Click the drop-down arrow to the right of the "Numbering" button on the "Home" tab in the Ribbon, select a numbering style, and begin typing. ***Or***, begin the paragraph by typing an Arabic or Roman numeral, followed by a period or parenthesis (for Arabic), followed by the "Spacebar."
2. Press the "Enter" key twice to complete the list.

Other Types of Notes

Inserting Screen Snippings

Screen Snipping in Windows 10 captures an image of anything visible onscreen and saves it to the clipboard.

1. Display the content to snip.
2. Hold down the "Windows" key and press the "Shift" and "S" keys.
3. Select a snipping option from the toolbar that appears.
4. **To define the area to snip for a "Rectangular Snip" or a "Freeform Snip,"** click, drag, and release the mouse. **To define the area to snip for a "Window Snip,"** click into the window. A "Fullscreen Snip" is automatically saved to the clipboard when "Fullscreen Snip" is selected.
5. Click into the page in OneNote where the content is to be displayed.
6. Click the "Clipboard" button on the "Home" tab in the Ribbon and select "Paste" from the menu. ***Or***, press the "Ctrl"+"V" keys.

Inserting Printouts from PDFs

Sequentially insert contents of a PDF file into a note, converting each page into an individual image. Non-PDF files are first converted to PDF. Attachments of any original files are also inserted. Attachments are copies and not linked to the originals. Changes made to one aren't applied to the other. **To open an attachment**, double-click it.

1. Click the "Printout" button on the "Insert" tab in the Ribbon. Printout
2. Navigate to the file in the "Open" dialog box, select it, and click the "Open" button.

Inserting Pictures

To insert pictures from your computer:

1. Click the "Pictures" button on the "Insert" tab in the Ribbon and select "From File."
2. Navigate to the picture by double-clicking the folders at the right in the "Open" dialog box.
3. Click to select the file and click the "Open" button.

To insert pictures from a camera:

1. Click the "Pictures" button on the "Insert" tab in the Ribbon and select "From Camera."
2. Allow OneNote to access your camera, if necessary.
3. **To take a photo**, click the screen. Repeat as desired.
4. Click the "Insert All" button.

To insert pictures from an online resource:

1. Click the "Pictures" button on the "Insert" tab in the Ribbon and select "From Online."
2. Type a keyword into the Bing Image Search text box in the "Online Pictures" pane and click the "Search" button.
3. Scroll to the desired picture and click to insert it.

To adjust the size of an image, click the image to select it. Then, click and drag one of the corner resizing handles.

Inserting Audio Notes

Audio files added to OneNote pages are represented by an icon within a note container.

To insert an existing audio file:

1. Click the "File" button on the "Insert" tab in the Ribbon.
2. Navigate to the file by double-clicking the folders at the right in the "Open" dialog box.
3. Click to select the file and click the "Open" button.
4. Select either to "Upload file to OneDrive and insert link" or "Insert as attachment."

To record an audio file:

1. Click the "Audio" button on the "Insert" tab in the Ribbon. Recording immediately begins.
2. **To stop recording**, click the "Stop" button on the "Recording" tab that appears in the Ribbon.

To play an audio file:

1. Double-click the file's icon on the notebook page. ***Or***, hover with the mouse over the icon and click the "Play" button that appears to the left of the icon. ***Or***, click the file's icon to select it and click the player control buttons on the "Audio" tab in the Ribbon.

Adding Hyperlinks & Email Addresses

Links to other OneNote content, external websites, and email addresses can be applied to any text or image. Web addresses automatically convert to hyperlinks when typed.

1. **To link to OneNote content**, right-click the destination notebook, section, page, or content, and select "Copy Link to [Destination]" from the menu.
2. Select the text or image to convert to a link. ***Or***, **to create a new link**, click into the desired location.
3. Click the "Link" button on the "Insert" tab in the Ribbon.
4. Type a full web address (e.g. www.teachucomp.com) or email address beginning with "mailto:" (e.g. mailto:info@domain.com) in the "Address" field. ***Or***, paste content from Step #1. **To change the link's displayed text**, edit the "Text to display" field.
5. Click the "Insert" button.
6. **To open a link attached to an image**, hold down the "Ctrl" key while clicking the image.

Attaching Other Types of Files

1. Click the "File" button on the "Insert" tab in the Ribbon.
2. Navigate to the file by double-clicking the folders at the right in the "Open" dialog box.
3. Click to select the file and click the "Open" button.
4. **To insert an icon that represents the file**, click "Insert as attachment" in the dialog box that appears. ***Or***, select a different attachment option.
5. **To open the file in its native application (e.g. Word, PowerPoint)**, double-click the file's icon.

Sending to OneNote

The "Send to OneNote" feature sends printouts from other applications to OneNote. The content is converted into an image. The content's text can be searched in OneNote, but not edited.

1. Select the "Print" command in the other application.
2. Select "OneNote for Windows 10" from the drop-down list of printers in the "Print" dialog box.
3. Click the "Print" button.
4. Select the notebook's section or page. ***Or***, navigate to a different location by clicking selections under "Other location."
5. Click the "OK" button.

Other Application Integrations

Inserting Outlook Meetings

1. Click the "Meeting Details" button on the "Insert" tab in the Ribbon.
2. Sign in with the appropriate Microsoft or other account in the "Meeting Details" pane, if necessary.
3. Click to select any of the current day's meetings displayed in the panel. ***Or***, click the "Today's Meetings" drop-down to navigate to a different date in the calendar that appears, then select the desired meeting.
4. Type meeting notes into the "Notes" section of the meeting details that appear on the notebook page.

Sending Notebook Pages via Mail

Send a static copy (screenshot) of the current page in an email.

1. Navigate to the page to send.
2. Click the "Share" button at the right end of the Ribbon.
3. Click the "Send a copy" link at the bottom of the "Share" pane.
4. Click "Mail" in the "Share" window and select an email account, if necessary.
5. Enter the email address(es) of the recipient(s) in the "To" field and a subject into the "Subject" field of the new email message window that is displayed.
6. Click the "Send" button in Mail.

Tables

Inserting Tables

1. Click in the position on the page where the table is to be inserted.
2. Click the "Table" button on the "Insert" tab in the Ribbon.
3. Drag over the grid and click to define the number of columns and rows.
4. **To advance to the next cell in the table**, press the "Tab" key.

To create a table on the fly:

1. Click in the page where the table is to be inserted.
2. Type the first column heading's text and press the "Tab" key. The new table appears.
3. Type the next column heading's text and press the "Tab" key. Repeat for each column.
4. After the last column, press the "Enter" key.
5. Enter data into a cell and press the "Tab" key to advance to the next cell. **To advance to the next row**, press the "Tab" key in the last cell of a row.

Modifying Table Columns and Rows

1. **To select, delete, insert, or modify a column or row**, first activate the table by clicking into a cell.
2. Click the "Table" tab that appears in the Ribbon.
3. **To modify columns and rows**, click into the table into a related cell. The buttons on the "Table" tab directly relate to the position of the cursor in the table (e.g. To delete a a row, click into any cell in that row and click the "Delete Rows" button in the Ribbon).
4. **To select the entire table or specific columns, rows, or cells**, click the "Select" button in the Ribbon and choose from the drop-down of selection options.

Formatting Tables & Table Data

1. **To adjust the width of a column or the table itself**, hover over the right edge of any column (or the table) until the cursor turns into a double-sided arrow. Click, drag and release to adjust the size.
2. **To adjust the height of a row**, click at the end of the content in a cell within the row and press the "Enter" key.
3. **To hide or display the table lines**, click the "Hide Borders" button on the "Table" tab in the Ribbon.
4. **To apply cell shading**, select the cell(s), click the arrow to the right of the "Shading" drop-down in the Ribbon and select a color.
5. **To format table data**, select the data or cells, click the "Home" tab in the Ribbon, and click one of the alignment choices in the "Paragraph Formating" drop-down. ***Or***, use any of the other formatting buttons in the Ribbon (see "Formatting Text" instructions).
6. **To sort table data**, click into the column by which to sort the table, click the "Sort" button in the Ribbon, and click to sort in ascending (A-Z) or descending (Z-A) order. **To include the header in the sort**, first select the "Include Header" option from the drop-down and then sort.
7. **To move an entire row's contents**, hover over the row and click and drag the icon that appears to the left of the row, once the cursor turns to a four-sided arrow.

Writing Tools

Creating Handwritten Notes & Drawings

1. Click the "Draw" tab in the Ribbon.
2. Click to select a pen style from the choices in the Ribbon (e.g. Black Pen tool).
3. **To customize the pen tool**, click the pen again and make color and size selections in the drop-down.
4. **To add a pen**, click the "Add Pen" button in the Ribbon, select to add a "Pen," "Pencil," or "Highlighter," and make color and size selections.
5. Click "Draw with Mouse or Touch," if necessary.
6. Write or draw with a stylus pen or the mouse.
7. **To erase any mistakes**, click the "Eraser" tool in the in the Ribbon and click on the *edge* of the writing/drawing. **To customize the "Eraser" tool**, click the button again and make choices.
8. **To convert a simple hand-drawn shape (square, circle, triangle, etc.) into a perfect preset one**, click the "Ink to Shape" button in the Ribbon and draw the shape.
9. **To modify a handwritten note or drawing**, first select it by clicking the "Select Objects or Type Text" button in the Ribbon (if necessary), and then clicking anywhere on the *edge* of the writing/drawing. A dotted line appears around the selection. Use the tools in the Ribbon to modify.
10. When done, click the "Select Objects or Type Text" button in the Ribbon to switch back into typing mode, if necessary.
11. **To convert handwriting to typed text**, select the handwriting and click the "Ink to Text" button in the Ribbon.

Inserting a Shape

1. Click the "Draw" tab in the Ribbon.
2. Click the "Shapes" drop-down in the Ribbon and select a shape.
3. Click, drag and release to draw the shape.

Deleting Handwritten Notes & Drawings

1. Click the "Select Objects or Type Text" button in the Ribbon. ***Or***, click the "Draw with Mouse or Touch" button (if necessary) and then the "Lasso Select" button.
2. Click and drag across or around the object(s).
3. Press the "Delete" key.

Tags

Adding Tags to Notes

Tags are visual identifiers used to identify content that fits into specific categories. Tags help organize content, remember important tasks and even locate specific content based on the tags attached to it. Tags can be applied to any type of content in OneNote.

1. Select the text or object to tag.
2. Click the "Home" tab in the Ribbon.
3. Click the arrow to the right of the "Tag" button in the Ribbon and select a tag from the menu. Clicking the "Tag" button instead of its drop-down arrow will automatically apply the "To-Do" tag.
4. **Or,** select the text or object to tag, or right-click the note container and click the "Tag" drop-down button in the Mini Toolbar. Select a tag.

Creating and Deleting Custom Tags

To create a new custom tag:

1. Select the text or object.
2. Click the "Home" tab in the Ribbon.
3. Click the arrow to the right of the "Tag" button in the Ribbon and select "Create New Tag" at the bottom of the list.
4. Enter a name in the "Tag name" field of the "Create a Tag" pane.
5. Click the "Featured" or "All Icons" link and then click an icon to select it.
6. Click the "Create" button.

To delete a custom tag:

1. Click the arrow to the right of the "Tag" button in the Ribbon and select "Delete Custom Tag." Select the tag to delete and click "Yes" to confirm.

Searching in OneNote

Searching for Tags

1. Click the "Search" button to the left of the Notebooks List.
2. Type a tag name in the search box and press the "Enter" key. ***Or***, select a tag under "Tags" in the drop-down list.
3. Select a location to search from the drop-down ("All Notebooks," "Current Notebook," etc.).
4. Click the "Tags" tab. The search results appear below.
5. **To jump to any tag displayed in the pane**, click it.

Searching for Text

1. Click the "Search" button to the left of the Notebooks List.
2. Type the text to find and press the "Enter" key. ***Or***, select a choice under "Recent searches" in the drop-down list.
3. Select a location to search from the drop-down ("All Notebooks," "Current Notebook," etc.).
4. Click the "Pages" tab. The search results appear below.
5. Click on a result in the search pane to jump to its page. The searched text will be highlighted.

Using Researcher

Use Researcher to locate articles, reliable sources and content for research projects. Explore and research the material related to your content and add it to your notes without leaving OneNote.

1. Click the "Researcher" button on the "Insert" tab in the Ribbon. Researcher
2. Type a topic into the search bar in the Researcher pane, then press the "Enter" key.
3. **To see more information on a topic**, click a result. **To return to results**, click the "Back" button.
4. **To refine search results**, select an available tab ("Websites," "Journals," "Books," etc.).
5. **To insert the result's URL into the note**, click its "Add to page" button.

Formatting & Viewing Pages

Formatting Page Backgrounds

1. Select the "View" tab in the Ribbon.
2. **To change the background color**, click the "Page Color" button in the Ribbon and select a color from the drop-down. **To remove a background color**, select "No Fill." Page Color
3. **To add rule or grid lines**, click the "Rule Lines" button in the Ribbon and make a selection from the drop-down. **To remove grid lines**, select "None." **To add the rule lines by default**, check the "Always Create Pages with Rule Lines" command at the bottom. Rule Lines

Changing Notebook Views

1. Select the "View" tab in the Ribbon.
2. **To enlarge or reduce the content of a page**, click the "Zoom Out" or "Zoom In" button in the Ribbon. **To further zoom**, continue to click the buttons.
3. **To expand the view of the content to fill the entire page**, click the "Page Width" button in the Ribbon.
4. **To revert to the default view**, click the "Zoom to 100%" button in the Ribbon.

Proofing & Printing

Checking Spelling

As you type, OneNote displays a red wavy line under words it thinks are spelled incorrectly.

1. Right-click on the word and choose from the "Proofing" command suggestions, if available. ***Or***,
2. If correct, choose "Ignore" or "Add to Dictionary" (to ignore spelling in all notebooks).

To hide spelling errors while working:

1. Click the "Settings & More" button in the upper-right corner of OneNote and select "Settings" from the drop-down.
2. Select "Options" from the menu.
3. Scroll down to "Proofing" and click the "Hide Spelling Errors" toggle button.

Printing

1. Click the "Settings & More" button in the upper-right corner of OneNote and select "Print" from the drop-down.
2. In the "Print" dialog box, select a printer, pages to print, the number of copies, and any other desired print settings.
3. Click the "Print" button.

Sharing & Collaborating

Creating a Shared Notebook

Notebooks can be shared with other people with permissions set to allow them to either edit or only view the notebook.

1. Click the "Share" button at the right end of the Ribbon. Current people and their permissions are listed under "This notebook is shared with" in the "Share" pane that opens. Share
2. **To share the notebook**, type one or more email addresses of the people with whom to share the current notebook in the "Type email addresses" field. Separate multiple addresses with a comma or semicolon.
3. Select a permission from the drop-down to allow invitees to edit or only view the notebook.
4. Click the "Share" button. An email is sent to the invitees with a link to view the notebook in OneNote online. Share
5. **To re-send the email to the invitee, change their permissions, or stop sharing with them**, click their name in the list and make a selection.

Turning Synchronization Off/On

By default, notebook synchronization to the cloud is turned on. Simultaneous changes made by others to shared notebooks are saved automatically.

1. Click the "Settings & More" button in the upper-right corner of OneNote and select "Settings" from the drop-down.
2. Select "Options" from the menu.
3. Under "Sync notebooks automatically," near the top of the pane, click the toggle button to turn synchronization on or off. On

Manual Synchronization

To sync a notebook once:

1. Click the "Saved offline (auto sync is off)" notification at the right end of the Ribbon.
2. Click the "Sync now" button in the drop-down.

Or

1. Right-click on the notebook title tab in the Notebooks List.
2. Select "Sync" and then either "Sync This Notebook" or "Sync All Notebooks" from the menu.

Editing & Reading Shared Notebooks

When others contribute to a shared notebook, the section's name is bolded on the section's tab in the Notebooks List and the specific page names are bolded, indicating changes exist that have not yet been read. Once the content is read, the section and page names become un-bolded.

To view the content provider's name and change details:

1. Right-click the author tag (author's initials) displayed next to changed content.
2. View the change details at the bottom of the menu.

To hide or show all content provider author tags:

1. Click the "View" tab in the Ribbon.
2. Click the "Hide Authors" toggle button in the Ribbon. Hide Authors

Keyboard Shortcuts

Working in OneNote

Open a notebook	**CTRL + O**
Create a Screen Clipping	**WINDOWS+SHIFT+S**
Create a new link	**CTRL+ K**
Add a new page at the end of the current section	**CTRL + N**
Create a new subpage	**CTRL+ALT+SHIFT+N**
Create a new section	**CTRL + T**
Search all open notebooks	**CTRL + E**
Go to the next section	**CTRL + TAB**
Go to the previous section	**CTRL + SHIFT + TAB**
Go to the next page	**CTRL + PAGE DOWN**
Go to the previous page	**CTRL + PAGE UP**
Go to the first page in section	**ALT + HOME**
Go to the last page in section	**ALT + END**

Touch Actions

Using a Touch Interface

Click or Double-Click	**Tap or Double-Tap**
Scroll	**Drag or Swipe**
Select text	**Double-Tap, then drag Selection Handle**
Right-Click Menu	**Touch and hold for box & release. Tap drop-down arrow**

ISBN 9781941854662